AF614405

B 11 Battery, R.A.,

Now the 13th Battery, R.F.A.

DARTMOOR 1873.

The History

OF THE

13th Battery, Royal Field Artillery

From 1759 to 1913

Major H. MARRIOTT SMITH, R.F.A.

The Naval & Military Press Ltd

published in association with

FIREPOWER
The Royal Artillery Museum
Woolwich

Published by
The Naval & Military Press Ltd
Unit 10 Ridgewood Industrial Park,
Uckfield, East Sussex,
TN22 5QE England
Tel: +44 (0) 1825 749494
Fax: +44 (0) 1825 765701
www.naval-military-press.com

in association with

FIREPOWER
The Royal Artillery Museum, Woolwich
www.firepower.org.uk

In reprinting in facsimile from the original, any imperfections are inevitably reproduced and the quality may fall short of modern type and cartographic standards.

CONTENTS.

The History of the 13th Battery Royal Field Artillery from 1759 to 1913.

CHAPTER I.

EARLY YEARS.

1759. THE initial failures of the 7 Years' War were followed in 1759 by a rapid succession of Naval and Military victories. Under the inspiring guidance of the elder Pitt, England renewed her strength, and every quarter of the Globe saw her soldiers and sailors triumphant. The Battle of Plassey had established her dominion in Bengal. Throughout India her power had already surpassed that of the Moguls. Hawke wrung from the tempests of Quiberon Bay a dramatic conquest for the British Navy. On the continent of Europe the astonishing charge of the British infantry on the French cavalry had won the victory of Minden, while in North America the dying Wolfe on the Heights of Abraham bequeathed Quebec, and with Quebec, Canada, to his country.

Such were the events which attended the birth of our small Unit, now the 13th Battery of the Royal Field Artillery, destined to a life already long and eventful.

The 15th Hussars, the 16th and 17th Lancers, the Black Watch and a 3rd Battalion of the Royal Artillery were added to the Army in this year.

That Royal Regiment of Artillery, then 33 years old, now numbers 285 batteries and companies, all of which share the traditions of all that the Regiment has done. Fourteen of these are our seniors. Those of us who serve in any of the older units may and should have, without detriment to our loyalty to the whole, a particular and affectionate sentiment concerning the past of our own battery, and it is worth while to

1759. try to trace in the not too well kept records of the past what manner of men our predecessors were, what life they led and what they achieved. Nor will the picture be complete if we fail to consider their outward appearance.

It is not suggested that we older units are superior to our younger sisters. Rather are we proud that the old Regiment has been able again and again to produce children indistinguishable in efficiency from her older offspring.

This 3rd Battalion then, was formed from a nucleus of five companies of the first and second Battalions and 500 recruits. From this mixture emerged 10 companies, each known by its captain's name and subsequently numbered from 1 to 10.

There remain to-day the 1st, 4th, 5th, 6th, 7th and 8th Companies. These are now known as the 12th Battery R.F.A., the 101st Company R.G.A., the 13th Battery R.F.A., No. 3 Mountain Battery R.G.A. the 66th Company R.G.A.. and the 14th Battery R.F.A.

The establishment of our Company at its formation and of later changes is given in an Appendix. Of the 82 men there shewn as gunners, 20 were gunners properly so called and 62 were mattrosses. The gunners were highly skilled men, and vacancies were filled as they occured by selection from the mattrosses, who performed the less important duties in the service of the gun, but only if there was a recruit ready to enlist as a mattross. One or two of the mattrosses had a fictitious existence. Their names appeared on the pay-list as John Doe or Richard Roe. There was a muster every month when these names were solemnly called over with the others. Their pay was drawn by the Company Commander and appropriated to Recruiting charges, for which there was no allowance, and to Officers' Widows.

The men wore white stockings for walking out, and for parade long black splatter-dashes with 36 buttons apiece. There was some difficulty in persuading the hair of some men to grow long enough to admit of the tail being tied behind in the orthodox manner.

The soldier with inadequate locks was provided with a wig until 1770, when the brilliant inspiration of some economist substituted a false plait. No deception was attempted as to

1759. the nature of this adornment, for it was fastened to the collar of the coat and was not affected by the movements of the wearer's head.

There were seven Officers; a Captain-Lieutenant, a Lieutenant, a second Lieutenant and three Lieutenant Fireworkers. These gentleman wore a more splendid uniform than we do in this age. A three-cornered covered hat, gold edged, surmounted a full-sized wig, smaller wigs being worn off parades. A scarlet waistcoat hung half-way to the knees of the scarlet breeches. The long blue coat hung open to shew its scarlet lining, and the cuffs were of the same colour. Your dandy surreptitiously added such gold embroidery as he hoped might escape from censure. The fine frills of a cambric shirt appeared at neck and wrist. Black boots reached above the knee. A crimson sash and a silver gorget completed a somewhat bold colour scheme. A brass hilted sword and a fusee (or musket) formed the arms.

1764. Buff became the colour for breeches and waistcoats for all ranks in 1764.

Captain J. Jeffreys was in command of the Company at this time.

1768-1770. White facings came in in 1768 and the officer discarded his musket.

1777. Captain R. Chapman became the captain in 1777. A gunner at this time always went on duty with three rounds of ball cartridge.

It is sad to relate that no Irishmen were allowed to enlist.

For these early years practically no records have been found of our Company's stations or services.

Most of the 3rd Battalion was employed in the American War of Independence.

1782. We went back to red facings in 1782.

1790. About 1790 the rest of the Battalion went to the West Indies, where they saw much active service, but our Company seems to have remained at Woolwich.

1793. In 1793 were born the first of your brilliant younger sisters, the batteries of the Royal Horse Artillery.

1795. In 1795 the Company under Major Bentham moved from

1795. Woolwich to Canterbury. That pleasant cathedral town was to be their headquarters for twenty years. Thence they set out for the campaigns of Egypt, of Corunna, of Vittoria, and of Waterloo, and thither they returned during the intervals between these campaigns, familiar figures to the old streets, clean shaved, powdered and pig-tailed, wearing the blue tailed coat with its scarlet facings, the large cocked hat and plume, trim white breeches and long black splatter-dashes. The move was part of the defence scheme against threatened invasion of England, Canterbury being the centre of the circumference of the menaced coast line of Kent. In this year Major Bentham was promoted Lieutenant-Colonel but retained command of the Company.

A gunner's knapsack, when carried in marching order, contained four white shirts, a check shirt, six false collars, a canvas frock, a pair of canvas trousers, a leather cap, two pairs of shoes, a pair of black cloth gaiters, one pair of white and one of worsted stockings, two shoe buckles, a powder bag and puff (for the hair), a razor and shaving box, two shoe brushes, a cloth brush, a twin screw and worm, a brush and pillow, a leather stock, a rosette, a pair of knee breeches, a stock buckle, a large and small comb.

1799. In 1799 the officers were ordered to wear a sash round the waist, a white cross belt with a metal breastplate and one epaulette ; the sergeants were armed with a brass hilted sword, and the gunner with a carbine and bayonet.

CHAPTER II.

EGYPT.

1800. IN May 1800 the Company marched to Portsmouth to take part in an expedition then being organised. The rest of the Battalion was then in the West Indies.

Colonel Seward commanded three companies, which formed the Artillery of the force.

A commissary of Ordnance brought the gun equipment, which remained on his charge and under his management. A detachment of the corps of R.A. Drivers also came with horses. The wildest confusion reigned at Portsmouth, increased by the presence there of another expedition destined for Egypt.

Drafts were received from nearly every artillery unit in England to bring the Company to a War Strength of 5 officers and 120 men. There was friction with commanders of regiments about the allotment of battalion guns. There was trouble with the Board of Ordnance about accounts. There were difficulties due to the mystery which hung over the destination of the Expedition. As a matter of fact no plan had been adopted by the Cabinet. Now it was to be Belle Isle, now Spain, now Italy, now Portugal or even South America. However, on May 25th the Artillery embarked in high spirits, but, after anchoring at Spithead, the transports only sailed up Southampton Water, where the soldiers' ardour was damped by an order to disembark. This afforded opportunity to the Board of Ordnance to aggravate the sorely tried Company Commander by initiating new disallowances, in connection with the change from ships' rations and pay to land rations and pay and back again. Fortunately only a few days were spent on shore. The expedition then sailed under Sir James Pulteney, 10,000 strong. They sighted the Port of Ferrol on the 24th August with a Spanish Fleet at anchor just inside the harbour.

1800. Covered by the fire of the men-of-war, the troops, with their guns, disembarked and gained some advantage over the Spaniards who opposed them. The General, however, was impressed by the strength of the Forts and at the preparations made to receive him. The troops were called off and embarked the same evening. The guns, ammunition boxes, etc. were loaded under the Commissaries of Ordnance in such a disorderly manner that subsequently no one piece was found fit for immediate service. It was remarked at the time that such duties should be left to artillery officers, and that each company should have its own epuipment, a consummation not really reached until 1849. Equally desirable was the permanent allotment of horses and drivers.

Vigo was then reconnoitred, but nothing could be effected there.

After this, the troops sailed to Gibraltar, where the Company landed on 19th September. Captain Beavor took over command from Lieut.-Col. Bentham, who, however, accompanied the expedition. Considerable re-organisation of personnel took place here. The drivers were sent to Lisbon and thence to England. On 27th October the transports sailed to Minorca, then the British Headquarters in the Mediterranean. Here Sir Ralph Abercromby took command. His force now numbered 12,000 men, intended to co-operate with Austria against Napoleon in Italy. England and Austria confronted France and Spain, while the Northern Confederation, consisting of Russia, Sweden and Denmark maintained an unfriendly and menacing neutrality.

The French held Egypt and Malta. Their naval force in the Mediterranean, though inferior in numbers, was active and troublesome.

Napoleon was crossing the Alps to fall upon the rear of the Austrian Army in Italy.

England was engaged in a struggle with Tippoo Sultan in the East Indies, and with the French in the West Indies. The problem of the English Cabinet was, as always, to find a suitable point at which to apply the small striking force available for offensive operations.

The prestige of the Army was low, as that of the Navy was

1800. high. 10,000 British Troops had been kept idle in and about the Mediterranean for two months.

On 10th June the Austrian Commander had sent an urgent appeal for the speedy arrival of the British Force. It was too late. On 14th June the catastrophe of MARENGO put an end to a disastrous Campaign, and the Austrians agreed to evacuate Italy south of the River Po.

Sir Ralph Abercrombie now sailed to Malta, arriving on 30th October. Here the campaigning equipment was overhauled. The list of deficiencies includes camp kettles, canteens and haversacks, while the tents had no poles. It was found that the guns had howitzer cartridges, a trouble not so serious as it might have been. The powder was re-weighed, and the soldier's wives, then an inseparable adjunct of a British Army, even on active service, re-sewed it in flannel cases.

Major Cookson's company, which lay alongside us, received from England a contractor of stores who could not even write. This, doubtless, amused us more than it did him. The officers were encouraged to engage Maltese servants by the grant of an allowance of one shilling a day should they do so. One Maltese demanded eighty pounds a year. "Do you know, my friend," said his prospective master, "that you ask more than is given to a subaltern officer, who must live like a gentleman, and expose himself, moreover, to all the severities and dangers of the Service?" "Ah, Sir," replied the suave domestic, "I do, indeed, know their distress, and I pity the poor gentlemen from my heart."

Malta was unhealthy. Half the gunners were down with fever. The soldiers embarked on 10th December, and on the 17th the great fleet of transports sailed under convoy from the beautiful Grand Harbour.

The 30th December saw the fifth disembarkation, this time at Marmara Bay in Asia Minor, opposite the Isle of Rhodes. The objective approached by this succession of knight's moves was now known. The French Army of Egypt, 26,000 strong, composed of the veterans of Castiglioni, of Arcola, of Lodi, of the Pyramids, standing secure upon the valley of the Nile, was to be assaulted in its stronghold. To the formidable nature of the enemy was added the difficulty of the country. No wood, no

1800. roads, few supplies, shortage of water and a burning sun. A busy time ensued for the gunners in Marmara Bay. The forests were ransacked for spars, saw pits were dug, and an arsenal sprung up, in which the artillery equipment was adapted to its work in the desert.

1801. Litters were made for the 6 pounders of different sizes, some to be carried by camels, some by horses and some by men, but all composed of two long skids, connected by cross-pieces. The gun or ammunition box was slung in the centre. Hand-carts were also made, poles substituted for shafts in the limbers, and broad treads fitted to the wheels. The ammunition was sorted into loads of sixteen complete rounds, and special cases were made for each half load. Gangways were made, and disembarkation was practised with such success that the guns were oftener ashore more quickly than the infantry. A gun crew on these occasions consisted of 25 men of the Royal Navy and 15 of the Royal Artillery. Small horses of bad quality arrived from Constantinople. Our 6 pounders had teams of six.

Then the English harness was all too big. The whole had to be taken to pieces; neck collars were replaced by breast collars, chain traces by ropes, while the rest of the gear was re-sewn.

Thus the shores of the Levant hummed with British industry, and the preparations which should have been made in Woolwich Arsenal were carried through in Asia, by the industry and ingenuity of British sailors and soldiers.

Meanwhile our placid allies, the Turks, looked on and kept their fast of Ramadan.

On the 23rd of February the force set sail, now 16,500 strong. On the 1st March, the fleet cast anchor in ABOUKIR Bay, among the wrecks of the French Fleet destroyed by Nelson, two and a half years before, at the battle of the Nile. The Foudroyant's cable fouled the sunken hull of the French Flagship L'ORIENT. The weather remained stormy until the 8th March. The low sandhills were crowned by 2000 French with 12 guns. At length, on the 9th March, the signal was given, and 150 boats formed on a front of one mile, rowed fast to the African shore through water foaming with bullet and round shot. The soldiers sat silent on the thwarts. The sailors rowed

1801. standing. Many boats sank, but the rest pushed on and reached the land; 5500 men and 14 guns landed in 10 minutes. They were charged by cavalry before they had time to form. Sternly repelling the attack, the infantry formed line and stormed the sandhills, capturing 8 guns. The French loss was 300, the British 500, mostly incurred before landing.

The next three days were spent in landing stores.

On the evening of March 12th the Army advanced and invested the Castle of Aboukir. On the 13th the enemy, now 6000 strong, were attacked in a formidable position covering Alexandria and driven back into the town.

The English lost 1200 men, the French 500. Aboukir was bombarded, and surrendered on the 19th. Abercrombie said of the gunners, "Difficulties were overcome which at first sight appeared insurmountable."

On March 21st the French, now in equal numbers, attacked with impetuous gallantry. The English suffered from an inferiority in guns and cavalry. After a confused and desperate battle, the French were driven from the field. During this, the battle of Alexandria, both gun and musket ammunition ran short, and the men actually threw stones at the enemy. The French lost 3000 men, the English 1500, and Sir Ralph Abercrombie was mortally wounded.

The conduct of the splendid British infantry has rarely been surpassed. Yet the British Artillery attracted great attention by the precision of their fire and the steadiness of their conduct. After the battle the miserable Turkish horses failed to move the guns, so that an advance and the fall of Alexandria were of necessity postponed.

On May 7th the new Commander, General Hutchinson, left a small force to contain Alexandria, and moved against the French in Cairo. During this march, the gunners were afforded unusual opportunities of displaying endurance and skill, and nobly they bore themselves. Boats, mules, oxen were requisitioned. No obstacle could stop them. The guns were up with the Army when it reached Cairo, which capitulated on May 20th. On June 24th Sir David Baird arrived with 8000 troops, having accomplished the feat of crossing the desert from Suez.

1801. The troops then marched north, and on August 17th active operations were begun against Alexandria.

On August 22nd General Menou made a determined effort to drive off the English Army. The brunt of the day fell on the Artillery and the advanced corps. "The celerity with which the guns were brought up was a remarkable instance of zeal, as they had to be carried over almost inaccessible rocks." "The proceedings against Alexandria showed to what a pitch of perfection the British Artillery had arrived," says Steward. The Battery on the Green Hill opened at 6 A.M. on the 26th. By mid-day the enemy were silenced and the batteries destroyed. On the west the tower of Marahout was struck by a shell four feet from the ground. Each succeeding shell struck the same spot until a large hole was made through the masonry. The building fell into the ditch and the Fort surrendered.

Alexandria itself capitulated on August 31st.

25,000 French soldiers evacuated Egypt under the Convention. The British Force at no time numbered more than 24,000; 1250 guns were taken from the French.

The greatness of this achievement shed lustre on British arms. They alone of all European soldiers had shewn themselves able to compete on equal terms, nay, against odds, with the veterans of France. The loss of Egypt wrung a passionate imprecation from Napoleon, who thus saw his cherished, though chimerical, dreams of Eastern Empire swept away. Nor was the campaign soon forgotten. It was with the cry "Remember Egypt" that Moore encouraged the 42nd Regiment at the crisis of Corunna, and it was heard again at Waterloo.

1802. On 16th November our Company was ordered home, disembarked at Portsmouth in July 1802, shortly after the peace of Amiens, and proceeded to Porchester, and, in August, to their old quarters at Canterbury.

By General Orders Oct. 31st.–Nov. 1st, 1803, the Officers, N.C.O's and men of the Company were given the distinction of wearing in their regimental caps the "Sphinx" with the word "Egypt," an honour still borne by the infantry regiments who took part in this campaign.

A scheme was inaugurated to concentrate the 3rd Battalion

1803. in Canada, but was frustrated by the recurrence of hostilities with France on the 6th May.

Minora canamus.—The officers were allowed to substitute blue pantaloons for the unserviceable white ones for campaigning and off parade. The strength of the Company was reduced to 75.

1805 A peaked cylindrical hat with plume and brass ornament in front was introduced for all ranks, though the officers continued to wear the cocked hat until 1812.

In 1805, the year of Trafalgar, occasion was found to issue an order that the feathers in the hats of Corporals, Bombardiers and Gunners were not to exceed 10 inches in height, nor those of the officers and sergeants 13 inches.

1808. In 1808 the War Office found time to reduce those of officers and sergeants also to a height of 10 inches.

On August 1st of this year, queues were directed to be discontinued and hair to be cut short, an order which the delighted soldiers obeyed with so much alacrity that, when a counter order arrived, it could not be obeyed. The pig-tails had gone and the picturesque powder and uncleanly pomatum were things of the past, though the waiters at the Woolwich mess wear powder on their hair to this day.

CHAPTER III.

CORUNNA.

1808. ON September 7th the Company was constituted a field brigade for active service by the addition of a detachment of R.A. Drivers with horses, 6 light six pounders and ammunition waggons, like Noah's Arks on wheels in appearance, with the following additional carriages: Forge Wagon, Spare Wheel Wagon, 2 Store Carts, one Captain's Cart. The latter carried the office boxes and "the jolly captain's shirts and stockings."

The R.A. Driver of the period was not a success. He had only ceased to be a waggoner and had not become a soldier. A few years previously his uniform was a smock frock, a tall hat with a plume and a carter's whip.

At this time his appearance when newly equipped was more military. He wore white pantaloons, black leather gaiters, a blue stable jacket and a jockey cap.

In the Peninsula he often contrived to lose some of his clothes, sometimes his boots, and on one recorded occasion his pantaloons.

In appreciating the difficulties of an artillery company not the least to be considered is that which was occasioned by a body of men, not of the best class, with no particular bond of union with the gunners, whose efficiency depended so much on the driver's exertions.

"The scourge of the Army" one irate gunner called them. It was not altogether their fault. Indifferently officered, their pay in arrears, short of rations, badly clothed, transferred from company to company and from gun to pontoon, it was not surprising that they were a source of trouble in a field brigade.

They bear no relation to the drivers of to-day, than whom no finer body of men exists in the service. Let those who have

1808. seen them in action deny it if they can. The change is due to their incorporation in the battery, whose success is their success and whose failure their failure. The strength of the Company was raised to 4 sergeants, 4 corporals, 9 bombardiers, 3 drummers and 116 gunners. The officers were Captain A. Bean, 2nd Captain T. A. Brandeth, Lieutenants J. Darby, W. E. Malling and T. R. Cookson.

Early in September the Company embarked at Ramsgate for the Peninsular with the Division of Sir David Baird. The transports riding at anchor had to endure a severe gale on the night of the 9th. On the 10th the wind was adverse, and so continued until the 14th, when it blew a gale. The wind remained in the N.W. quarter until the 19th.

On the 18th orders were received to sail to Corunna.

On the 20th the Fleet set out, 300 sail in all.

On the 21st the wind compelled them to bear up for the Downs, but the ship which carried our brigade reached Corunna on the 8th of October.

The approach to that town is beautiful, high and picturesque hills closing each side of a deep bay.

The horses were swum ashore and the guns landed. More horses were received from England, mostly cripples.

Officers' horses were compulsorily taken for draft on payment. Eventually the guns and ammunition wagons were drawn by a motley collection of horses, mules and oxen.

The start was not propitious, but no doubt there were N.C.O's and men in the Company, who wore the Sphinx in their hats, and were able to remind the younger soldiers of the delays and disappointments which preceded the success in Egypt seven years before.

On 15th November the force marched 9 miles to Betanzos, a miserable townlet. A distant view was obtained of Ferrol, the scene of the abortive attempt in which the Company shared in 1800.

The march lasted from 10 A.M. to 4 P.M. slow going.

Next day, after a delay in getting forage and in pouring rain, Monte Santiago, 9 miles off, was reached at dusk.

On the 17th there was more rain, and Baalmonde was reached, 12 miles on.

1808. On 18th to Lugo by 4 P.M., 12 miles, where they halted until 21st.

On 23rd at Cacabelos, rumours of Spanish disaster were prevalent.

On 26th at Astorga, Captain Bean gave a dinner party to his friends. The Brigade remained halted until 1st December. Orders were received to fall back on receipt of news of the destruction of Spanish Armies of Castanos and Palafox. Our Brigade was with the rearguard, also 7th Light Dragoon, 43rd and 95th Foot, and B Troop R.H.A.

On the 2nd December women and sick were sent to the rear.

On the 4th from Bembire they marched to Ponferrade.

On the 5th Captain Bogue breakfasted with Captain Bean.

The orders for retreat were cancelled, and junction with Sir John Moore's force at Tilwara resolved upon.

The Artillery was reorganised. Our Brigade became one of three with right of Army under Colonel Cookson.

On the 21st deep snow lay on the ground during the cavalry affair at Sahagun, at which Captain Brandeth was present. Baird's Division with our Brigade joined Sir J. Moore's force.

On the 25th the troops marched to the attack of Soult, when news was received that Napoleon at the head of 100,000 men was marching from Madrid to intercept the Army. The retreat began on the same day, and was continued in bitter cold and with cruel suffering.

Already the British were cut off from Portugal, and it was possible that they might be anticipated at Benavente and cut off from Corunna also.

The retreat was marred by scenes of shameful disorder; 2600 stragglers were reported. Robbery and violence marked the trail of the main body.

Nov. But while hardship and forced marches relaxed the bonds of discipline of the main body, the rearguard, which from day to day withstood the onset of the pursuing French, held high the standard, not of valour alone, but of loyal obedience to orders. And beside Crawford's noble regiments of Light Infantry, stood, from time to time, Captain Bean with four of his six guns.

The other two joined the 4th Company of the 7th R.A.

1808. Battalion, now the 9th Battery R.F.A., under Captain Wall on the 30th November at Astorga.

Dec. With him they marched next day 31 miles to St. Romana, resumed their journey at 3 o'clock next morning, and halted at Cacabelos. On 3rd December they camped at Villa Franca, on the 4th six miles from Herreria, on the 5th at Constantino, on the 6th and 7th at Lugo, on the 8th and 9th at Barmonde. On the 16th they returned to Lugo, and on the 18th to Astorga. This division of the battery reached Corunna on the 8th January, and rejoined Captain Bean on the 11th. Meanwhile the other four guns remained with the rearguard. At Astorga the heavy baggage of the Brigade had been stored, and it had to be destroyed as they passed on December 30th. The road beyond was strewn with dead animals and the debris thrown away by the main body in their march.

1809. The rearguard was engaged at Constantino on January 6th,
Jan. and Captain Bean's guns were firing during the day. The troops were skilfully drawn up, and the French, though they lost 200 men, achieved nothing. The rearguard fell back to Lugo on the 6th; our guns were again engaged during the movement.

Here the whole Army occupied a strong position. At the report of the impending battle the stragglers of the main body thronged to rejoin the colours. A weak attempt made by Soult on the 7th was repulsed with a loss of 300 men. During the 8th the two Armies waited face to face. That night the British slipped away. But the old disorder marked the retreat of the main body. Heavy rain added to the confusion. Five miles only had been covered when the sun rose. Happily it was late on the 9th before Soult resumed his advance, and our rearguard was not overtaken until they reached the Ladra, half way to Betanzos. Next night the retreat continued, the rearguard covering Betanzos during the 10th. These two days cost the British 1000 men.

Captain Bean's Brigade marched into Corunna on 11th January, and with sad hearts the men embarked their equipment, but they were spared the bitter feelings with which the three remaining Artillery Brigades, on the night of the 16th, spiked their guns and hurled them over the cliffs into the sea.

During October 13th the men of the Company had congenial

1809 employment in blowing up a magazine of 12,000 barrels of gun-powder, a magnificent spectacle. The men-of-war in the harbour were rocked by the explosion.

On the 14th and 15th the men were engaged in destroying 50 guns and 20 mortars on the sea front of Corunna, under the orders of Major Beavor, who had commanded the Company in Egypt.

At 3 P.M. Soult attacked.

Men of the Company were employed under Lieutenant Cookson in carrying ammunition up to the guns, the fire from which was very heavy. Lieutenant Darby had embarked with the guns of the Brigade.

Soult was flung back with a loss of 1200 men, the British lost 800. Sir J. Moore fell in the hour of victory.

After the battle the Company, with the artillery companies now known as the 4th Battery R.F.A. and No. 3 Mountain Battery R.G.A., manned the guns on the land front of the Corunna fortifications under Major Beavor.

In the small hours of the 17th, the gunners in the central bastion were disturbed by the dull sound of picks and mattocks. A small party of infantry was digging a shallow trench on the ramparts. As the grey dawn broke and revealed torn filaments of sea mist driven inland by the south-west wind, a detachment of the 9th Regiment, bearing a body wrapped in a military cloak, passed silently by. When they reached the trench, they laid, by the light of a single lantern, all that was mortal of Sir John Moore in the hastily made grave. The solemn words of the funeral service were punctuated by shots from the French guns, which now opened fire on the shipping from the north side of the harbour.

> "Few and short were the prayers we said,
> And we spake not a word of sorrow.
> But we steadfastly gazed on the face that was dead
> And we bitterly thought of the morrow."

The embarkation of the troops had been in progress all night. Now the enemy's fire caused dreadful confusion. Some ships cut their cables—some went on the rocks and sank. By nightfall most had got out of the harbour, but it was not until

1809. the night of the 18th that Captain Beavor got his men on board with the rearguard. The last transports sailed on the 19th for England.

The voyage was tempestuous in the extreme. The men were half naked, starved, worn out with toil and misery. Many died on the voyage. So in gloom and with every appearance of disaster ended the second adventure of the Company in the Peninsula. None the less the wound inflicted on Napoleon was severe. He lost heavily in the pursuit. Just when he had Spain at her last gasp he had been compelled to relax his grip. The guerilla warfare burst out afresh and was never subdued. The contest continued to drain his strength and to add fresh laurels to British arms, until the tide of war swept back his legions and the British armies surged over the Pyrenees into the plains of Southern France.

CHAPTER IV.

VITTORIA TO WATERLOO.

1809. THE shattered remains of the Company returned to Canterbury to recover in their old home from the effects of all they had undergone.

1810-1813. In January 1810 they moved to Battle, and later to Ringmer, where Captain Bean handed over the command to Captain Hutcheson, just before the Company embarked for Lisbon at Portsmouth on 4th February.

The other officers were :—

> Second Captain Bentham.
> Lieutenant C. A. Moore, killed at Geuve de Moulan 1814.
> Lieutenant R. Manners, killed at Ligny 1815.
> Lieutenant J. Christie, killed at New Orleans 1814,

so that all three subalterns were killed in action in the next two years.

An officer's field kit included an octagonal hair trunk, a camp table, two camp stools, a bedside carpet, and a camp bed with curtains.

The Company reached Lisbon on March 19th and marched on 21st with 30 musket ball cartridge carts with horses, for the right of the army.

They were with the reserve artillery and musket ammunition at Aguilar de Campos on June 20th, under orders to march to Villacayo, near Vittoria, *via* Reinosa.

On June 17th 200 mules under a commissariat officer were sent to join the brigade at Sabugal. Two deaths occurred during this month. The battery records state that the Company was present at the battle of Vittoria, but no further details have been discovered. They were at Vittoria on 4th July, when large

1813. numbers of men were on detachment. They were at Algeria on 7th October, where Lieutenant Manners left the Company.

The presence of the Company at the second siege of Sebastian is also noted in the battery records and by Duncan, but they were apparently represented by a detachment only.

1814. On the 8th March next year the brigade was sent with the 4th and 7th Divisions under Marshal Beresford to Bordeaux in answer to a Royalist invitation.

The force arrived before the town on the 12th, when the French burnt some men-of-war building on the stocks and evacuated the town. One battalion of Conscripts surrendered. The British occupied the town amid the acclamations of the inhabitants.

April. On 4th April the force under Lord Dalhousie crossed the Garonne to attack 2000 French, whom they defeated, taking 300 prisoners.

On 8th April the news of Napoleon's abdication reached the South of France and put an end to the war.

July. The Company embarked for England in July and returned to Canterbury.

1815. On the escape of Napoleon from Elba, the Company embarked for Belgium and reached Ostend in May 1815.

Captain Hutcheson was placed in command at that place, where the headquarters of the Company remained until after the Battle of Waterloo. Only a detachment was engaged in the
June. battle, where fell their old commander Captain Beavor; also Lieutenant Manners, a former subaltern, was killed at Ligny.

The rest of the Company joined the Allied Forces after the battle and marched to Paris, which they reached in August. They probably took part in one or more of the minor sieges of fortresses in France, as in 1819 Captain Hutcheson was awarded a brevet majority for his services.

The British horse and field batteries were at this time the admiration of the Armies of Europe assembled at Paris. Veteran Commanders of every nation used to examine with insatiable interest the details of that admirable equipment, and were loud in their applause of the horses which drew and the soldiers who manned the Artillery of England.

CHAPTER V.

THE LONG PEACE.

1815. IN December 1815 the brigade became part of the army of occupation, and took up its quarters at St. Almond and remained there for a year.

1816. Then they moved to Valenciences on the Belgian Frontier, whence they returned to Woolwich in September 1819.

A black shako with a peak, gold-laced top and bottom, and blue grey trousers and gaiters were taken into wear.

1819. They there suffered from the reduction common to the British Army at that time.

The brigade was reduced from 160 men to 70, and from 122 horses to 36.

1820. A blue coatee with scarlet plastron and cuffs was worn, Hessian boots and tassels by the officers.

Annual practice was almost unknown.

There was nothing to work for at Woolwich.

Historic companies were disbanded. A few others dragged out a languid existence. Promotion there was none. Major Hutchesson commanded the Company for fifteen years.

1822. In 1822 the Corps of drivers was abolished, being in a worse state than the companies.

Thereafter the Company enlists its recruits as "Gunner-Driver."

One drummer was trained as a trumpeter, one man as a shoeing smith, one half of each company were to be trained to the care of horses as well as to other duties, and for all this 5 complete horses were allotted to each company!

1824. A long single breasted coatee and blue grey trousers with a red stripe was introduced in 1824.

1826. Woolwich was exchanged for Ireland in January 1826.

1827. In 1827 we have a picture of the gunner-driver. "Some had

1827. never been on horseback, could not put on the harness, hold the reins or groom a horse. Some nearly fell off in marching past."

Kind providence removed the Company in February 1827 to Gibraltar, whence they became a garrison company, instead of
1830. the travesty of a field brigade. In July 1830 Major Hutcheson was at last promoted and left for the Ionian Isles.

1832. In 1832 our Regiment was granted by King William the arms at present in use and the motto "Ubique, quo fas et gloria ducunt." All other distinctions, such as our Sphinx, ceased to be borne.

The uniform at this time consisted of an enormous shako with a white plume and cap lines, a double breasted blue coatee with red facings, blue grey trousers with a red stripe and two white cross belts.

1834. In 1834 the Company returned to Woolwich, then a stony-hearted step-mother to the Regiment, to take their share of Arsenal fatigues and other drudgery.

They spent four dull years there, and five at Manchester. At this time white trousers were sometimes worn in full dress. Drummers wore scarlet coatees.

1840. A drummer's knapsack held the following kit. Two linen shirts, one flannel shirt, a towel, two pairs of worsted stockings, a holdall, a bible and prayer book, a button stick and brush, a pair of shoe brushes, a tin of blacking, a cloth brush, a forage cap, a fatigue jacket, a pair of trousers and a pair of wellington boots.

1841. In 1841 the white trousers were discontinued, and Captain Ingilby took command.

1843. In 1843 the Company moved to Canada and spent one year
1844. at Quebec, and next year moved to Kingston.

1845. From 1845 the sergeants no longer carried halberds.

It is to be hoped that the following inducements to "fine young men" to enlist in the artillery were not wholly illusory. The recruiting sergeant undertook that they should be made gentlemen and treated accordingly. They were to be taught the Arts of Riding, Driving, Drawing, Fencing, Gunnery and the Mechanics, the making and use of gunpowder, sky rockets and other fireworks, and to cap all, by the power of the lever, to

1845. move a 42 pounder battering gun with the same facility as a *penny whistle.*

They were to wear a splendid uniform, and to be well mounted, to have light work and good pay, a canteen in which to see their friends and take a cheerful glass.

When at home, they were to have the best beef that Kent could provide, while a park and pleasure grounds, presumably the Woolwich Repository, would be a their disposal. They were to have opportunity to travel in Foreign countries, where wine was twopence a bottle, and would finally return to their friends with money, manners and experience.

If only half this was true, who would not 'list as a gunner?

1849. Captain Mundy succeeded Captain Ingilby in 1849.

1851. In 1851 the Company returned from Canada to Woolwich.

The serjeants' blue greatcoats were embellished with a scarlet collar.

Some slight progress had been made at the Regimental Headquarters in military instruction. Annual practice took place on Plumstead Marshes, subject to much interruption from passing ships on the Thames. Impatient company commanders would open a rapid and uninstructive fire when the range was clear, and so home to the dinner of "Kentish Beef."

Some years companies went to Shoeburyness to practice on the range acquired there in 1849. The effective range was 1000 yards for shell, and round shot were still the *pièce de résistance*, their function to carry terror and confusion into the rear ranks of the enemy's columns. Nine pounder batteries, fully equipped, were maintained in the grand depôt at Woolwich, and handed over to companies for training from time to time.

Gunners were only allowed to mount on the carriages for trotting past and driving drill, when the No. I commanded from the off limber box. When acting with other troops they were dismounted. The harness was of black leather and included blinkers. After a year at Woolwich the Company was sent to Ireland, and spent three years at Spike Island, Cork Harbour, Portobello and Ballingcollig.

The battery was one of the two grey field batteries, and very proud they were of their grey horses, which they retained until they embarked for India in 1873.

CHAPTER VI.

THE CRIMEA.

1853. IN 1853 the long peace was broken by the war with Russia. Captain Ormsby succeeded Captain Mundy.

1854. The Company reached Woolwich in October 1854, and there became "J" Battery of position, though still the 5th company of the 3rd Battalion. They were armed with three 32 pounder howitzers, firing shell only, and made of gunmetal. They weighed less than the 9 pounder guns. "J" was brigaded "V" Battery, now the 25th R.F.A., which was similarly equipped. The officers of "J" were Captain F. B. Ward, 2nd Captain N. C. L. Blosse, Lieuts. C. L. Tredcroft, A. C. Dyer and F. A. Wingate.

1855. Mar. At 4 A.M. on the 10th March the Battery was at the docks at Liverpool ready to embark on the steamer "Indian." No sailors had been on board for two days, nor had any arrangements been made for the embarkation. However, by 11.30 A.M., men, horses and guns were on board. From then, the battery only spent 13 years out of the next 56 at home.

Men and horses were overcrowded. Holes were cut in the deck, and wind-sails rigged to bring air to those horses accommodated near the engines. The "Indian" remained at anchor at the mouth of the Mersey until the morning of the 14th, when she put to sea in a gale of wind, still 200 tons short of the proper ballast. She, in consequence, rolled dangerously, and the horse fittings gave much anxiety. Two horses broke their backs, and many others were injured during the storm, which lasted for 3 days. They reached Gibraltar on March 21st, Malta on the 26th, Kulum in Asia Minor on the 31st, and camped at Scutari, 7 miles off.

April. Next day they re-embarked on the "Indian," and steamed eastwards between the coasts of Asia and Europe, sighting head-

1855. land after headland gay with pink almond blossom and the fresh green tints of early Spring. A fog hung over the Black Sea. The ship cast anchor in Kazatch Bay at 2 P.M. on April 7th, and in Balaclava harbour on the morning of the 8th.

During the 14th and 15th the horses were landed and the battery camped at Karani. Five horses in all were lost during the voyage and two during the first night in camp. On the 14th a subaltern and fifty men were sent to help to work the guns in the trenches. Six of these were wounded, five by the explosion of a magazine. Their behaviour was admirable, and a complimentary order was published respecting the "bravery and general conduct" of the new arrivals by the Officer Commanding the Right Attack. Rain fell heavily while the remainder were moving into camp, and the men and the grey horses were not looking their best when inspected by Lord Raglan on the 15th. He, however, said he had never seen so fine looking a battery, and moreover directed them to get their 32 pounder howitzers exchanged for 18 pounder guns. Now these heavy guns had intervened with decisive effeet at ALMA, and again at INKERMAN. Lord Raglan had a high opinion of them, and it was no small compliment to "J" Battery to be selected to handle these guns. They fired shot as well as shell, and weighed 42 cwt., exclusive of limber and ammunition. The guns were at the time in position in the defences of Balaclava under Sir Colin Campbell. Captain Ward, after a difficult interview, persuaded him to resign them, on promising to replace them by others, if required at any time. At a second interview, Sir Colin was at first very angry, but, with returning good humour, said he saw he had been done out of his guns by "a damned red-headed, oily tongued fellow from Woolwich." Now, our Commanding Officer's hair was certainly of a fiery colour, but, chuckled Sir Colin, so was Lord Raglan's. The Commander-in-Chief was also Master General of the Ordnance, and it was in that capacity that he had given orders to change the guns. Captain Ward did not, in the end, give Sir Colin any guns instead, and the conversation on this subject ended by his saying to Captain Ward that he had been done again.

The men made themselves comfortable and happy in camp, and, as is the custom of the British soldier to this day, usually

1855. broke into song when it rained. In wet weather the mud was fearful, but the slopes of the hills round Karani were covered with wild flowers. A spring of pure water bubbled up close at hand.

May On May 15th Omar Pasha, the Turkish Commander-in-Chief, who had heard of this fine battery, came over to see and admire it. The guns were drawn by 12 grey horses, four abreast, and their appearance was unusual and impressive.

June The 3rd bombardment took place on the 5th, 6th and 7th, June, when the mamelon was captured by the French. At this time the field batteries were mostly employed in taking ammunition down to the trenches—hot work sometimes. There the overworked Companies of Garrison Artillery, assisted by occasional detachments of Field Gunners, manned the Siege Guns under the envious eyes of the Field Artillerymen ; and won so much praise not only from our allies, the French, but from our great antagonist in SEVASTOPOL, General Todleben. The British in this engagement lost 1500 men, 104 of whom were gunners.

After this, frames and planks were issued to the battery, with which to build stables for the horses. These they constructed themselves, but, as they were not a success, being too small and too hot, only three were put up. A new equipment of improved 18 pounders weighing 38 cwt. arrived from England for "J" Battery.

July. Five men died of cholera during July.

Aug. On August 15th the French had four cavalry regiments with horse artillery behind the Fidioukine Hills, the Sardinians 15,000 men at Karani near Mount Hasfort, and the British their cavalry division at Kadekoi, with "J" and "V" Batteries at Karani. This position Prince Gortchakoff proposed to attack with the relieving army, then 70,000 strong.

On this day Captain Ward, who commanded the Reserve Artillery, reconnoitred Canrobert Hill, and reported that his guns could be taken up that or Mount Hasfort. No notice was taken of his report. Next day the storm burst, and the Russians attacked. Captain Ward received orders to bring up howitzers.

1855. He therefore reluctantly left his own battery behind and took "V" Battery with the 32 pounder howitzers with an escort of 2 squadrons of the Carabiniers to Mount Hasfort. The Russian attack was brilliantly beaten off by the Sardinians in the battle of Tchernaya.

It was from no fault of Captain Ward's that the battery did not get into action in this engagement. He received, however, the following letter written in French from the Commander-in-Chief of the Sardinian Army :—

"MONSIEUR LE COMMANDANT,

"It is a pleasant duty to have to thank you, Monsieur, and to tell you how much I appreciate your co-operation on the 16th, when your guns and mine joined in the defence of the positions so vehemently attacked by the enemy.

"I also congratulate you, Monsieur, on the admirable bearing of your men, and give myself the pleasure of hoping that on the first possible opportunity we may again have the pleasure of fighting side by side."

. . . . . .

Signed, "ALPHONSE LA MARMORA.

"KADAKOI, 8*th August*."

British Military etiquette was outraged that a letter from the Commander-in-Chief of an Allied Army should be sent direct to a mere captain of artillery—and Captain Ward's services on this day were for some time ignored. He received however in November due recognition, and was granted a brevet majority.

During the latter part of August, "J" Battery was attached to the Highland Division supporting the Sardinian right flank, and stood to arms daily an hour before dawn. The end of the siege was now in sight. Sevastopol was bombarded August 17th to 21st and again on September 5th.

Sept. On September 8th a successful assault was delivered and the Russians evacuated the fortress next day, but retained their

1855 hold on the other side of the harbour. The British loss was 2600, and that of the gunners 160. On September 9th "J" Battery received a draft of 56 men from home. The battery losses up to this date were 17 men by death from sickness, and 7 wounded, while 39 had been invalided. After the fall of Sevastopol, the battery moved to camp at Ramara close to the river. On its arrival it was reviewed by the new Turkish Commander, and he and his whole staff were effusive in their expression of pleasure at what they saw. At the end of September a party of the battery, who were fetching materials for the winter huts, were fired on by the Russians on the other side of the harbour, and three horses were killed. The men were kept hard at work preparing for the coming winter.

Oct. By the end of October the cold had become intense, and it was difficult to keep the inside of the huts above freezing point. The camp stood in a sea of mud whenever the thermometer rose.

Nov. A big review of all the horse, field and position batteries was held in November, and "J" Battery was again congratulated on all sides on its appearance and the rapidity with which the heavy guns were brought into action.

Dec. By Christmas, fires notwithstanding, the quicksilver in the hut thermometers had disappeared from sight, these instruments not being made to record temperatures below zero, Fahrenheit. Snow lay deep upon the ground, but the men and horses of the battery kept in good condition. Christmas dinner in the officers' mess included a turkey, a goose and a plum pudding, while the men had roast beef and plum pudding.

1856. Jan. On the 7th January the frost broke and the surroundings again became wretched. A plague of savage rats overran the camp. The Battery Sergeant-Major, a man 6 feet 3 inches in height and of stalwart build, returned to camp one night, his face pallid and contorted with terror. He had been attacked by some hundreds of these brutes on the road, and had escaped with difficulty. This non-commissioned officer was shortly afterwards promoted to a cornetcy in the Land Transport Corps. This month each officer and man gave a day's pay to Miss Nightingale's fund for the sick and wounded. The rain and sleet continually beat through the thin boarding of the huts

1856. and the men's blankets would be soaked by morning. Only 5 horses died during the winter. At the beginning of March hostilities were suspended and peace was concluded on the 30th. The field allowance of sixpence a day drawn by all ranks was instantly stopped.

Mar. The Army was in a high state of efficiency and not altogether pleased not to have opportunities of distinction in the coming spring. The troops everywhere fraternised with their gallant enemies. Picturesque groups of English, French, Italians, Russians, Armenians and Greeks thronged through the camp.

At the end of March a detachment of Miss Nightingale's nurses arrived to look after the sick. The Artillery Chaplain was bringing them up to camp in an ambulance when the mules took fright and upset the conveyance. All the men's devotion to these gallant ladies and distress at the accident could not prevent them from laughing at the Irish Chaplain's consternation and excited description of the scene. "The ambulance was for all the world like a pigeon pie with the legs sticking out at the top." No great harm was done, and their presence in the hospital brought relief to many sufferers.

The battery returned to Woolwich on 18th June 1856, and on the 4th July was, with the rest of the Artillery, reviewed by Queen Victoria on the Common.

The following General Order was published:—"Although only a few days have elapsed since their disembarkation, the good-working condition of the horses and the health of the men afford sufficient proof of the admirable system established in the Regiment. Despite the disadvantages of a sea voyage, the movements were performed with the precision of that noble Artillery, which under all circumstances has maintained its high character for perseverance, endurance and courage in siege and field."

Many of the leading features of Woolwich to-day were then existing. The great front of the Artillery barracks bounded one side of the barrack field, itself then bare of trees. The Royal Military Academy lay at the foot of Shooter's Hill. The tent roof of the Rotunda rose among the groves of the Repository. Southwards from the common lay a rural view of

1856. field and woods, now replaced by houses. Mortar practice then and long afterwards took place on the Common.

The Colonels Commandant ruled supreme and kept alive much tradition, and, it must be confessed, some military pedantry. The men were bearded when they came back from the Crimea; the beard was removed in the autumn of this year, but the whiskers and moustache remained.

CHAPTER VII.

THE MUTINY AND AFTER.

1857. IN May 1857 the Mutiny broke out in India, and on 18th June the Battery embarked for service there, bidding farewell to Woolwich, which had been their headquarters since 1824, as Canterbury had been during the last years of the eighteenth and early years of the nineteenth century.

Captain Dynely succeeded to the command in this year. "J" Battery landed at Calcutta on the 19th October soon after the fall of Delhi and the relief of Lucknow. The worst was over. There remained much hard marching; fighting, which became less and less frequent, and in which the importance of Artillery steadily diminished. The campaign was to continue for two years yet—to continue through cold weather, hot weather and rains without intermission. After disembarking, the Grey Battery, then armed with 9 pounders, marched up the Ganges to Benares to join Colonel Corfield's force, then based on Sasseran and operating against Kunwar Singh in the Jugdespore jungle.

Little record has been found of "J's" doings—but the work must have been analogous to that performed during the closing years of the South African War, with the addition of a tropical sun and tropical disease. A small peaked cap with a curtain behind was an inadequate protection from the one, while the latter took full toll of the lives of the artillerymen.

1858. Lieutenant Poulden died at Sasseran in May 1858, and Major Dynely at Calcatta in the same year. Captain Henry succeeded to the command of the Company.

On May 14th an engagement of some importance took place at Azimguhr, at which the guns of "J" Battery were commanded by Lieutenants Franklin and Mitchell.

1859. On 25th March 1859, we find the battery at Bootwall in Nepal, and in action on the 28th-30th. It also took part in the affair of Lou Gocutt on July 18th, under Colonel Kelly, where two of the gunners were wounded. The heat during this operation was terrible, and all suffered from exhaustion.

In April of this year came to an end the battalions which had existed, though loosely connected, for 150 years. They were replaced by an organisation of one Brigade of Horse Artillery and fourteen Field and Garrison, and "J" Battery became, for one year, the third battery of the 14th Brigade, which consisted of nine of the batteries of field and garrison artillery stationed in Bengal.

The Brigade was commanded by a Colonel. Non-commissioned officers were promoted by him in the brigade, and all correspondence passed through his hands. The brigade also had a Colonel Commandant, who lived at Woolwich and appointed the Adjutant.

1860. The circle of Commandants of the widely distributed brigades concentrated round the fire of the Woolwich Mess must have been rather overwhelming for the newly joined officer.

In 1860 our Battery joined the Nepal Field Force under Colonel Kelly. On the conclusion of operations, they marched to Fyzabad, when they became the 1st Battery of the 11th Brigade.

1862. In 1862 the Battery received another title, "A" Battery, 11th Brigade, and in 1863 became "B" Battery of the same brigade on change of station to Lucknow. Here they spent five
1867. years, returning home in '67, where they occupied the huts at Shorncliffe.

The uniform now worn was the tunic, cut lower in the collar than at present, and booted overalls strapped inside. The horse carried his rider's kit in the wallets and a valise behind the saddle, both covered by sheepskin for the men, and lambskin for the officers edged with red. The round forage cap was worn in undress, and the busby in full dress.

1868. The Battery moved to Aldershot under Captain Shakerly in August 1868, and to Hilsea in 1869.

1871. The left half Battery was sent to the cavalry barracks at Exeter in February 1871.

This year the Battery was reunited at Aldershot for autumn manœuvres, and obtained for experimental purposes their first breech loading equipment, the 16 pounder R.B.L. Guns. Teams of 8 horses were used. (*See frontispiece.*)

After manœuvres the four left subdivisions went to Exeter, and the right section to Hilsea, and the next year this section also marched to Exeter.

1872. Major C. Tupper now commanded the Battery. The routine of a mounted parade would begin with marching past in three different formations—then one or two changes of front without gaining ground followed by the sword exercise. After this ritual the guns would be brought into action. Rapidity in opening fire was more considered than accurate laying. Then the guns would be dismounted, and with these slung under the limbers and the wheels and carriages tied on top, the cavalcade returned to Barracks.

1873- The Battery took part in the autumn manœuvres on Dart-
1874. more in 1873, and in 1874, under Captain Jenkins, embarked for India on the troopship "Crocodile," arriving at Bombay on 21st February after a passage of 40 days. After the then customary stay at Deolali, they were stationed at Barrackpore. A cork helmet had been introduced during their 6 years stay at home—also Kahki clothing, and White for full dress in the hot weather.

1877. The Battery became "B" Battery, 4th Brigade. The 4th Brigade was considered the smartest of the brigades of field artillery and a nursery for budding horse artillerymen. At this time it must be remembered that excellence in turnout was given an undue prominence, and that shooting was relegated to a secondary position. A false standard and a false pride in certain portions of the regiment.

1878- In 1878 B 4 marched to Allahabad—a march of 42 days, and
1881. in 1881 to Rawal-Pindi, a march of 97 days.

1884. In 1884 they marched to Meerut, a 56 days' march.

1886. In 1886 the Battery embarked 67 strong at Bombay on the troopship "Euphrates," and proceeded to Limerick. While they had been in India the busby had been superseded by the blue

1886. helmet. Knee boots and pantaloons had displaced the booted overall. The collar of the tunic had become higher, and the tunic itself tighter and shorter.

1887. In 1887 the Battery were given 12 pounder B.L. guns. This gun was, at the time of its introduction, the best in Europe, and its type remained unaltered for 20 years.

1888. The Battery went to Clonmel in 1888, and became the 13th Field Battery R.A. in 1889. From this year may be dated the revival of the attention devoted to gunnery. Practice which had hitherto taken place against targets, 9 foot square, became more realistic. The impetus came from India, and rapid progress took place there and at home.

Competitive practice was started and served a useful purpose, though at the cost of excessive rivalry between batteries.

1890. The battery went to Hilsea in 1890, and to Aldershot in 1893.

1893. In 1893 they were chosen to carry our an interesting experiment, to test the endurance of the men and equipment. They were in action from 8 A.M. to 8 P.M, pausing only to change position; 970 rounds were fired. The 12 pounder used black powder fired case, common and shrapnel. In the normal method, the guns were fired in rotation from flank to flank. All ranks stood to attention in their places. Teams were usually up with the guns. The gunners wore long sword bayonets and short black gaiters over their trousers.

1896. In 1896 the Battery exchanged the 12 pounder for the 15 pounder, which fired cordite and shrapnel shell and case only, the necessity for common shell being diminished by the introduction of a field howitzer in this year. This year they moved to Dorchester.

1897. In 1897, in consequence of the altered political conditions following the Jameson Raid, the 13th, 67th and 69th Batteries were made up to War Strength and went to Natal. The 13th embarked on the Transport "Dilwara," under Major P. Crampton, on May 15th, and reached Durban on June 15th. Only one horse died on the voyage, and the remainder landed in excellent condition. They railed to Pietermaritzburg, whence they marched to Ladysmith, arriving on July 8th. At Lady-

1897. smith they were encamped. The expectations of active service came, for the time being, to nothing. The camp was sandy and uncomfortable. The horses suffered from horse sickness and sand colic.

1899. In 1899 the Field Artillery was organised in brigade divisions, the 13th with the 67th and 69th Batteries becoming the 1st Brigade Division R.F.A. This association has proved a happy one, despite the proverbial difficulties of a company of three.

CHAPTER VIII.

SOUTH AFRICAN CAMPAIGN.

1899. Sept. DURING September 1899 precautionary measures were taken for the defence of the Natal Frontier on account of the strained relations between the British and Transvaal Governments, and on September 25, the 13th and 67th Batteries marched to Sunday's river and on the 26th to Glencoe.

Oct. On October 9th an ultimatum was sent to Great Britain and on the 11th began the South African War, destined to last for two years and nine months. The next day the families of the battery were sent to Maritzburg. On October 15th the Transvaalers occupied Newcastle, and on the 19th the communications of the force at Glencoe with Ladysmith were cut at Elandslaagte.

The column, of which the 1st Brigade Division, now complete with the three batteries, formed the artillery, was at this time camped in an amphitheatre of six miles diameter, within cannon shot of Talana and Lennox Hills to the East. The dangerously isolated position of the force in this locality was dictated by political and not by military expediency.

While a large body of the enemy were moving on Elandslaagte a force of 4000 Boers, after a night march, seized Talana Hill on the morning of the 19th, and about 5.30 A.M. their guns opened fire on the camps. The artillery horses were down at water and the men of the force had just fallen out after the morning parade. The 67th Battery opened fire from their Gun Park on the lower slopes of Talana Hill while the drivers brought back the horses. The 69th followed by the 13th hooked in under fire, and, trotting through the outskirts of Dundee into action on a knoll south of the town, opened at a

1899. range of 3600 yards, ten minutes after the first shell arrived in the camp. In fifteen minutes the Transvaal guns were silenced and withdrawn. The 13th and 69th Batteries at 8 A.M. moved northwards to cover the advance of the infantry against the eastern face of Talana Hill. At 7. 30 A.M. the infantry advanced from the Sandspruit. At 8 A.M. the 69th Battery came into action at 2400 yards against Talana, while the 13th on their right opened fire on Lennox Hill. At 11. 30 A.M. the artillery were ordered to cease firing and Talana was successfully assaulted. The guns now crossed the Sandspruit to a range of 1500 yards and were directed to open fire. From this new position it was not possible to see the top of the hill nor that part of it had been captured. The result was unfortunate, and our infantry had to evacuate the crest. The occupation was not completed until 1.30 P.M. The 13th and 69th Batteries then advanced rapidly to Smith's Nek and unlimbered in drizzling rain, just as the Transvaalers retired across their front, 1000 yards away. The Batteries were, however, through a misconception of the situation, not allowed to fire. The force withdrew to camp at dusk. One driver and two horses of the 13th had been wounded. The Dundee Station - Master, then 60 years old, supplied the men with refreshments during the day.

Next day General French disposed of the Transvaalers at Elandslaagte; but the situation still gave cause for grave anxiety. During this day the battery was in action all day, and opened fire at 5. 30 P.M. against the Boers moving on to Impati to the north. At 2 P.M. on the morrow the force moved to a position on the spur of Idumeni. Later, the 67th and 69th Batteries and Cavalry marched to Glencoe Pass and returned at night to Idumeni. At 9 P.M. the force marched southwards by the track leading to Helpmakaar, leaving their camp standing. They skirted Dundee, which was actually occupied by the Boers at the time. The retreat was begun none too soon, and so deep was the mud and so dark the night that by the dawn of the 23rd the force had only covered 10 miles. The 13th Battery was in position with the rearguard. The column halted from day-light until 10 A.M., when the retirement was resumed. The top of Beit's Pass was reached at

1899. 2.30 P.M., and the force bivouacked in the mud until midnight.

Next day saw our Battery still with the rearguard. The force here turned west to Ladysmith. The rearguard crossed the Washbank River early in the morning. They halted here, 30 miles from Ladysmith, until dark. During the day, the 24th, the enemy were reported to the north and guns were heard to the north-west. This was a force from Ladysmith trying to cover the withdrawal of the Dundee Force.

The Cavalry with the 67th and 69th Field Batteries went out to co-operate, but returned at 4 P.M. At 2 A.M. on the 25th the force marched to Sunday's River, which was crossed at 10 A.M. Six miles further on, the force halted until 6 P.M. The march was continued throughout the night, and on the 26th Ladysmith was reached in safety. The last twelve miles took twelve hours to accomplish. The rain had been heavy and the work almost continuous since the morning of Talana Hill.

There was, however, no rest for the Dundee Column. The infantry went on outpost, and on the 27th the battery joined General French at De Vaal's farm and returned on the 28th.

That evening and next day ammunition was drawn. The story that the Ordnance Sergeant remonstrated on the quantity, pointing out that the 1st Brigade Division had already used up more than their annual allowance, cannot be authenticated, but it was current soon after among the gunners with Methuen's Column on the Modder River.

Meanwhile the commandoes of the two States were at last closing in on Ladysmith. It was decided to strike one more blow at them, and a too elaborate scheme was drawn up. In accordance with this, the 1st Brigade Division moved off at 9 P.M. towards Lombard's Kop, and formed up under cover of Limit Hill until daybreak.

The 1st and 2nd Brigade Divisions deployed for action and the infantry advance began. The dispositions at dawn were not in accordance with the plan. The flank attack on Nicholson's Nek on the left miscarried, and the force making it was eventually destroyed. The commandoes of the Orange Free State

1899. were moving against the west of Ladysmith. The infantry engaged in the frontal attack were ordered to fall back. The troops in front of the 13th Battery, already deeply committed, suffered heavily as soon as they began to retire, and, broken by the heavy fire, retired rather rapidly across the plain. A machine gun was lost, and the veldt began to bear a resemblance to a stricken field. The enemy advanced boldly. A crisis was at hand; in vain did the 21st Battery, north of Lombard's Kop, pour shell upon the advancing Boers; the counter attack came on, spreading far to the north and east and the 21st had to fall back.

It is doubtful if ever in the long history of the 13th Battery a more splendid opportunity presented itself, and eagerly they seized it. They had already occupied three positions, each nearer to the enemy, and now, advancing at a steady trot, they unlimbered 1000 yards *nearer* the enemy than the broken infantry, and 700 yards from the nearest groups of Boers. Enfiladed by shell fire from the east, exposed to gun and rifle fire from the north, they stood proud and alone, the mark of every weapon that the enemy could bring to bear upon them. Two guns were swung round to fire to the east, the other four faced north. The destruction of the battery seemed only a matter of minutes, as it disappeared from the eyes of the anxious spectators in the columns of smoke and dust thrown up by bursting shell. The flashes of their guns alone showed that they still fought. Yet help was at hand; the 53rd Battery, not to be outdone in knightly prowess, galloped up into action on their right, and the two British Batteries stood, isolated and unsupported, until the withdrawal of the infantry was assured.

Then at last, and by order of General Hunter, who was present with the guns, the 13th withdrew. The limbers came steadily up; one driver still remembers that the dressing was perfect; the retirement began at a walk, as then laid down in the drill book; the subsequent trot was steady and collected. The Battery dropped into action again farther South. The Battery Sergeant-Major had been mortally wounded, three gunners and four drivers were wounded, five horses had been killed and five wounded.

Then came the turn of the 53rd Battery to go. The hail of

1899. shell continued. One limber was smashed by a shell and the gun was left behind. A wagon was upset. The remaining five guns came into action beside the 13th. There remained two groups alone in the plain. The one, a wagon limber of the 53rd limbering up the gun left behind, and the other a group of men and horses where the overturned wagon was being righted. The gun came into action in its proper place in the battery and the wagon was brought safely back.

A new line of battle had been formed. The fire of the two batteries had killed the impetus of the counter-attack. The force fell slowly back, the batteries retiring in succession from the left, and occupied the line round the town which they were to hold for so long. The guns were the last to leave the field. So ended the mournful Monday of the battle of Ladysmith.

Nov. The Officer Commanding the 60th Rifles sent a letter to the battery to thank them for the services they had rendered his regiment in covering their retirement on the 29th. Queen Victoria wrote to convey her regret at the death of so good a soldier as Battery Sergeant-Major Garner, who had served in the Battery since 1869.

The 13th Battery was allotted to the defence of Section A of the defences at Helpmakaar and Devon Post, east of the town and north of the Klip River, and helped to construct the fine defences of this portion of the line. This section had the smallest field of fire and was exposed to shell fire from the north, east and south.

By the beginning of November, the investment of Ladysmith was completed by the enemy. The bombardment began on the 1st and continued throughout the siege. On the 17th, three guns which showed signs of wear were exchanged for new ones. The Battery, or portions of it, took its place from time to time in various movements, which were carried out by night. On the 25th the meat ration was reduced.

Dec. The horses were continually a mark for the enemy's guns. A horse was killed on November 18th, and another wounded on December 8th. On the 22nd there was no more hay for them.

1900. Jan. On January 6th at 3 A.M. heavy rifle fire was heard at Wagon Hill to the southward. The right section opened fire on the Boers closing in on Limit Hill, while the other two sections engaged the enemy attacking Devon Post. They were under continuous fire from the heavy guns on Bulwana and Caesar's Camp. At 4 P.M. one section moved out to engage the enemy on Caesar's Camp, but the heavy rain and darkness prevented them from opening fire. The dangerous attack on Wagon Hill was beaten off. One horse of the battery was killed on the 6th and three were killed and two wounded on the 17th. On the 30th horseflesh was issued as a ration. Portions of the Battery were in action from time to time.

Feb. The siege became unendurably monotonous. On the 10th February the horses' grain ration was reduced to two pounds, and the grazing was exhausted. Some grass was cut and given to the horses. By the 23rd the horses were so weak that the greatest difficulty was found in getting the guns to the tops of the hills.

On the 28th Ladysmith was at last relieved, having endured a siege of four months.

Mar. On March 1st Lieut.-Col. Pickwoad, commanding the 1st Brigade Division, was wounded while with the force operating against the retreating Boers. On the 3rd the Battery helped to line the streets as the relieving force marched in, and on the 4th a thanksgiving service was held.

On the 12th the Battery moved to camp near Observation Hill. Fresh horses were obtained, and the men's health, which had suffered from their privations, rapidly improved during the remainder of the month.

April. On April 6th the Battery marched to Modder Spruit and camped at Elandslaagte on the 7th. On the 10th the enemy fired into the camp. The force was under arms
May. from then until the night of the 11th. From that time until early in June the Natal Field Force was engaged in desultory operations in the northern angle of Natal. The 13th Battery had its full share of marching and counter marching.

June. On the 7th of June the force was concentrated for more

1900. active measures. The 13th and 69th Batteries accompanied General Wynne's 11th Brigade on the left in the attack upon Botha's Pass, a neck in the Drakensberg, 6000 feet above the sea, on the 8th. The artillery was skilfully handled, and the infantry seized the heights without much difficulty. The 13th Battery had fired 62 rounds. The Battery then mounted the steep ascent of the pass. Leaving the left section in action at the top, the Battery accompanied the 18th and 19th Hussars in pursuit.

It returned at night to the top of the pass, where the bivouack was bitterly cold, the men having no cloaks or blankets.

It was now necessary to clear the enemy from the vicinity of Laing's Nek, where they lay on the flank of the proposed advance. The Battery moved northwards on the 9th, and on the 10th came into action at Gans Vlei against the enemy retiring to Alleman's Nek. On the 11th this pass was stormed, the Dorset Regiment leading the attack. The Battery was with the Lancaster Regiment on rearguard. After this action they accompanied the central column during the advance, and reached Volksrust on the 12th. They were in action in a few small engagements, and were under fire more than once during the following days. On the 30th they were sent back to Mount Prospect and Ingogo, to be employed on the line of communications.

July to Dec. Work was incessant and was generally performed by sections. The country round Wakkerstroom and Ingogo became familiar to them. A pom-pom was at one time attached to them, also a naval 12 pounder. Cattle was collected from the country round, and a few rounds were occasionally fired.

1901. Convoy duty was frequent. The centre section worked from 8th of February to 17th March between Castral Nek and Piet Relief. On the 15th February the horses of the centre section at Ingogo, except four for the two guns, were sent to Artillery working in the Eastern Transvaal under General French. The other two sections continued their monotonous round of small and indecisive engagements. In June Major Dawkins left the Battery.

1901. The right section joined Pultenay's column on August 10th.
Aug. It was now decided to send one Brigade Division to India, and
it fell to the lot of the 1st, having been longest in the country, to
go. The headquarters of the Battery received its orders on the
Oct. 15th, reached Newcastle on the 29th, and on October 1st handed
over the horses, ammunition and transport. On the 3rd they
entrained, reaching Durban on the 21st, after twice detraining,
and embarked on the steamship "Armenian" as escort to
Boer prisoners. The Battery had been in South Africa
for five years, and for two years on active service. Twelve
N.C.O.'s and men were killed or died of disease during
the war.

Nov The "Armenian" sailed on 3rd November and reached
Bombay on the 26th. Next day the Battery left
by train with their prisoners for Saharanpur, which
they reached on the 30th. Here the prisoners were handed
over, and the Battery proceeded to Nowgong to be stationed.

1902. Major Lachlan took command at the New Year. Distinguished Conduct Medals were presented to B. S.-M. Glasgow, B. Q.M.S. Reeve and Gunner Callow at the Delhi Durbar by H.R.H. the Duke of Connaught.

1903. In 1903 the cumbrous title of Brigade Division was abolished, and the 1st Brigade Division became the 1st Brigade R.F.A. In March the Battery lost some men from cholera and had to go into cholera camp. In November they were prevented from going to manœuvres by a bad outbreak of malaria.

1904- After two years at Nowgong, the Battery moved to Mian
1905. Mir, a year later to Ferozepore, and in November 1905 to
Rawal-Pindi.

1906- In 1906 the establishment of horses was raised to 230, the
1907. extra drivers being natives. Next year they were armed with
new 18 Pounder Q.F. Equipment. In May 1907 there were
serious riots, and for two days the Battery was on guard over
Cantonments.

1909- In 1909 they went to Campbellpore on change of stations,
1910. and on 10th October 1910 marched for Nasirabad, arriving on
December 30th. They were instantly sent out to practice

marching. After manœuvres they marched to Neemuch, arriving on February 15th, having covered 955 miles by road. 1911.

Sailing from Bombay in S.S. "Rewa," in December 1912, they arrived at anchor in Southampton Water just as the church bells on shore could be heard ringing the New Year in. 1912

[APPENDICES.

APPENDIX "A."

BATTERY MOVEMENTS AND STATIONS.

1795 to 1800.	May.	Woolwich.	
	20th May.	Canterbury.	
	25th May.	March to Portsmouth.	England.
		Spithead and Southampton.	
	June.	**Affair of Ferrol.**	
		Voyage to Gibraltar.	
	22nd June.	Gibraltar.	
	11th July.	Voyage to Minorca.	
	August.	Minorca.	Mediterranean.
	10th Dec.	Malta.	
		Blockade of Valetta.	
1801.	21st Jan.	Voyage to Asia Minor.	
	23rd Feb.	Marmara Bay.	Asia Minor.
	16th Nov.	**Campaign of Egypt.**	Egypt (8 months).
1802.	July.	Malta and Voyage Home.	
	August.	Porchester.	
1803.	June.	Canterbury.	
1808.	February.	Dover.	England (6 years).
	September.	Canterbury.	
	8th Oct.	Voyage to Corunna.	
1809.	18th Jan.	Northern Spain.	Spain (4 months).
		Campaign of Corunna.	
	December.	Canterbury.	

BATTERY MOVEMENTS AND STATIONS—*continued.*

1813.	January.	Battle.	England (4 years).
	February.	Ringmer.	
	18th March.	Voyage to Lisbon.	
	23rd March.	Lisbon.	
	23rd July.	**Campaign of Vittoria.**	Spain (1 year).
1814.	14th Jan.	**Campaign in Northern Spain.**	
	March.	**Campaign in Southern France.**	
	July.	Bordeaux.	France.
1815.	May.	Canterbury.	England.
	July.	**Campaign of Waterloo.**	Belgium (1 month).
	August.	Paris.	
	December.	St. Denis.	
1816.	October.	St. Almond.	Northern France (3 years).
1818.	October.	Valenciences.	
1819.	September.	Woolwich.	
	December.	Weedon.	England (5 years).
1824.	1st Dec.	Woolwich.	
1826.	February.	Island Bridge.	
	December.	Charlemont.	Ireland (3 years).
1827.	21st Feb.	Island Bridge.	
	March.	Voyage to Gibraltar.	
1834.	October.	Gibraltar.	Spain (7 years).
1838.	December.	Woolwich.	
1843.	March.	Manchester.	England (9 years).
	May.	Woolwich.	
	August.	Voyage to Canada.	

BATTERY MOVEMENTS AND STATIONS—*continued.*

1845.	May.	Quebec.	Canada (4 years).
1849.	17th May.	Kingston.	
	30th June.	Voyage Home.	
1851.	January.	Woolwich.	
	December.	Spike Island.	England (1 year).
1852.	November.	Cork Harbour.	
1854.	April.	Portobello, Dublin.	
	July.	Spike Island.	Ireland (3 years).
	September.	Ballincollig.	
	October.	Woolwich.	
	December.	Sheerness.	England (3 years).
	7th March.	Woolwich.	
1856.	May.	Crimea.	
		Siege of Sevastopol.	Russia (1 year).
1857.	18th June.	Woolwich.	England (1 year).
	October.	Voyage to India.	
		Indian Mutiny. Nepal Frontier.	
1860.	January.	Bengal.	
	February.	March to Fyzabad.	
1863.	January.	Fyzabad.	
	February.	March to Lucknow.	
1867.	February.	Lucknow.	India (11 years).
1868.	April.	Voyage Home.	
1869.	August.	Aldershot.	
1871.	September.	Aldershot and Hilsea.	
1873.	September.	March to Devonport.	England (5 years).

BATTERY MOVEMENTS AND STATIONS—*continued.*

1874.	January.	Devonport.	
	March.	Voyage to India.	
1878.	April.	Barrackpore.	
1882.	February.	Allahabad.	India (12 years).
1884.	December.	Rawal-Pindi.	
1886.	9th April.	Meerut.	
	16th Nov.	Voyage Home.	
1888.	26th Sept.	Limerick.	Ireland (2 years).
1890.	27th Sept.	Clonmel.	
1893.	13th July.	Hilsea.	
1896.	30th May.	Aldershot.	England (6 years).
1897.	15th May.	Dorchester.	
	9th June.	Voyage to South Africa.	
	7th July.	Marched from Durban to Ladysmith.	S. Africa (5 years).
1901.	15th June.	**South African Campaign.**	
		Voyage to India.	
1903.	March.	Nowgong.	
1904.	19th Feb.	Mian Mir.	
	20th Dec.	Ferozepore.	India (11 years).
1909.	3rd Jan.	Rawal-Pindi.	
1910.	9th Oct.	Campbellpore.	
1911.	15th Feb.	March to Neemuch.	
1912.	10th Dec.	Neemuch.	
1913.	1st Jan.	Voyage to England.	
		Edinburgh.	Scotland.

APPENDIX "B."

BATTERY ESTABLISHMENTS.

Year.	Officers.	Staff-Sergeants and Sergeants.	Corporals.	Bombardiers.	Artificers.	Drummers or Trumpeters.	Gunners.	Drivers.	Native Drivers.	Total.	Horses or Mules.	Remarks.
1759	7	3	3	8	—	2	82	—	—	105	—	Seven Years War.
1763	6	2	2	4	—	2	38	—	—	54	—	Peace.
1771	5	2	2	4	—	2	42	—	—	57	—	Peace.
1782	6	4	4	9	—	2	91	—	—	116	—	War of American Independence.
1783	6	4	4	9	—	2	43	—	—	62	—	Peace.
1801	5	4	4	7	—	3	93	—	—	98	—	Egyptian Expedition.
1803	5	3	3	6	—	3	70	—	—	90	—	Peace of Amiens.
1808	5	4	4	9	—	3	116	—	—	141	—	Corunna Campaign.
1803	5	4	4	9	—	3	103	—	—	128	—	Vittoria Campaign.
1815	5	4	4	9	—	1	139	96	—	258	158	Waterloo Campaign.
1819	5	2	3	4	—	2	59	15	—	90	15	Peace.
1826	5	2	3	4	—	2	59	4	—	79	5	Peace.
1830	5	2	3	4	—	2	59	2	—	77	4	Peace.
1848	5	2	3	4	—	2	59	30	—	105	56	Peace.
1855	6	8	6	6	10	2	*182	—	—	220	150	Crimea.
1859	†4	—	—	—	—	—	†88	—	—	†92	†89	Mutiny.
1897	5	9	6	10	4	2	89	50	—	175	138	South Africa.
1906	5	9	7	20	4	2	78	53	40	229	230	India.
1912	5	9	7	20	5	2	78	53	13	192	173	India.
1913	5	7	4	4	7	2	60	53	—	142	60	Scotland.

* Gunner Drivers. † Strength only.

APPENDIX "C."

PAY OF VARIOUS RANKS OF 13TH BATTERY R.F.A. FROM 1759 TO 1913.

YEAR.	1759.	1797.	1806.	1849.	1860.	1868.	1870.	1878.	1881.	1890.	1899.	1902.	1906.	1913.
COUNTRY.	England.	England.	England.	Canada.	India.	England.	England.	India.	India.	Ireland.	South Africa.	India.	India.	Scotland
RANK.	S. D.	S. D	S. D.	S. D.	S. D.	S. D.	S. D.	S. D.	S. D	S. D.	S. D.	S. D.	S. D.	S. D.
Major,	—	15 0	—	—	*26 4	16 11	16 0	*32 0	*32 0	16 0	19 0	*32 0	*32 0	16 0
Captain,	10 0	10 0	11 1	12 2	*21 4	14 1	12 1	*21 1	*21 1	11 7	14 7	*21 1	*21 1	11 7
2nd Captain,	6 0	7 0	11 1	11 1	*19 2	12 2	11 0	—	—	—	—	—	—	—
Lieutenant,	5 0	5 0	6 10	6 10	*11 5	6 5	6 5	*12 6	*12 6	6 10	9 10	*12 6	*12 6	6 10
2nd Lieutenant,	4 0	4 0	5 7	5 7	*9 2	5 7	5 7	*10 1	*10 1	5 7	8 7	*10 1	*10 1	5 7
Lieut. Fireworker,	3 0	4 0	—	—	—	—	—	—	—	—	—	—	—	—
Staff-Sergeant,	—	—	—	3 2	3 9¼	3 11¼	3 11¼	3 10	4 2	4 2	4 5	5 0	4 11	4 11
Sergeant,	1 7¾	2 2	2 5	2 8	2 10	3 0	3 0	2 11	3 2	3 2	3 5	4 0	3 11	3 11
Corporal,	1 6½	2 0¼	2 2	2 2	2 2	2 4	2 2	2 6	2 6	2 6	2 9	3 4	3 3	3 3
Bombardier,	1 4½	1 10¼	2 0	2 0	2 0	2 2	2 0	2 3	2 3	2 3	2 6	3 1	3 0	3 0
Acting Bombardier,	—	—	—	—	—	—	—	1 11	1 11	1 11	1 10	2 5	2 4	2 4
Drummer,	0 9½	1 3¼	1 3¼	1 3¼	—	—	—	—	—	—	—	—	—	—
Trumpeter,	—	—	—	—	1 3¼	1 5¼	1 2¼	1 2	1 2¼	1 2¼	1 5½	2 0½	1 11½	1 11½
Mattross,	0 9½	—	—	—	—	—	—	—	—	—	—	—	—	—
1st Gunner or 1st Class Gunner,	1 1¼	1 7	1 7	—	—	—	—	—	—	—	—	1 9½	1 5½	1 5½
Gunner,	—	1 3¼	1 3¼	1 3¼	1 3¼	1 5¼	1 2¼	1 2¼	1 2¼	1 2¼	1 5½	1 5½	1 5½	1 5½
Layer or Signaller,	—	—	—	—	—	—	—	—	—	—		2 0½	1 11½	1 11½
Shoeing Smith,	—	—	—	—	—		—	1 11	1 11	1 11	1 10	2 5	2 9	2 9
Fitter,	—	—	—	—	—	—	—	—	—	—	—	—	2 9	2 9
1st Class Driver,	—	—	—	—	—	—	—	—	—	—	—	2 0½	1 11½	1 11½
Driver,	—	1 3¼	1 3¼	1 3¼	1 3¼	1 5¼	1 2¼	1 2¼	1 2¼	1 2¼	1 5½	1 5½	1 5½	1 5½
Native Driver,	—	—	—	—	—	—	—	—	—	—	—	0 7	0 7	—

* Consolidated.

APPENDIX "D.'

COMMANDING OFFICERS.

1759. Not known.
1764. Captain Josiah Jeffreys.
1777. „ Richard Chapman.
1782. „ Francis M. Dixon.
1783. „ Robert Douglas.
1794. „ John A. Schalon.
1794. „ William Brutham.
1801. „ Robert Beevor.
1801. „ George Beane.
1812. „ Thomas Hutcheson.
1830. „ William Bell.
1841. „ John Bloomfield.
1841. „ W. B. Ingilby.
1841. „ Robert Burn.
1849. „ P. H. Mundy.
1851. „ J. W. Ormsby.
1854. „ P. F. G. Scott.
1854. „ F. B. Ward.
1857. Captain E. E. Dynely.
1858. „ S. M. Grylls.
1858. „ G. C. Henry.
1859. „ B. Lawson.
1862. „ P. W. L'Estrange.
1867 „ G. J. Shakerly.
1871. Major A. E. de V. T. Tupper.
1873. „ E. C. W. Raynsford.
1875. „ H. de G. Warter.
1879. „ A. E. Garnault.
1885. „ A. J. Pearson.
1888. „ G. M. Flint.
1892. „ E. A. Lambert.
1897. „ P. J. R. Crampton.
1899. „ J. W. G. Dawkins.
1902. „ E. M. Lachlan.
1910. „ A. U. Stockley.
1912. „ H. R. W. M. Smith.

www.ingramcontent.com/pod-product-compliance
Ingram Content Group UK Ltd.
Pitfield, Milton Keynes, MK11 3LW, UK
UKHW041844190726
13854UKWH00002B/714

9 781845 740498